Orangutans

Patricia Kendell

HODDER
Wayland

An imprint of Hodder Children's Books

Alligators Chimpanzees Dolphins Elephants
Giraffes Gorillas Grizzly Bears Hippos
Leopards Lions Orangutans Pandas Penguins
Polar Bears Rhinos Sea Otters Sharks Tigers

 © 2003 White-Thomson Publishing Ltd

Produced for Hodder Wayland by White-Thomson Publishing Ltd

Editor: Kay Barnham
Designer: Tim Mayer
Consultant: Peter Ramshaw – Head of the Asia Pacific Team at
  WWF-UK
Language Consultant: Norah Granger – Senior Lecturer in Primary
  Education at the University of Brighton
Picture research: Shelley Noronha – Glass Onion Pictures

Published in Great Britain in 2003 by Hodder Wayland,
an imprint of Hodder Children's Books.

The right of Patricia Kendell to be identified as the author of this
Work has been asserted by her in accordance with the Copyright,
Designs and Patents Act 1988.

J599·883
1212307

All instructions, information and advice given in this book are
believed to be reliable and accurate. All guidelines and warnings
should be read carefully and the author, packager, editor and
publisher cannot accept responsibility for injuries or damage arising
out of failure to comply with the same.

Photograph acknowledgements:
BBC Natural History Unit 1 & 22 (Anup Shah);
Bruce Coleman 9 (Alain Compost), 29 (Gerald S Cubitt),
11 (Fredriksson), 10 (Werner Layer), 20 (Jorg & Petra Wegner);
FLPA 19 (Minden Pictures), 18 (Jurgen & Christine Sohns);
HWPL/Orangutan Foundation 17, 26; Nature Picture Library
16 (Neil Lucas); OSF cover & 6 (Daniel Cox), 4, 7 (Mike Hill),
25 (Harold Taylor), 5, 8, 12, 14, 23, 27, 28 (Konrad Wothe);
SPL 15 (Renée Lynn); Still Pictures 21 & 32 (Compost/Visage),
13, 24 (Dario Novellino).

British Library Cataloguing in Publication Data
Kendell, Patricia
  Orangutans. – (In the wild)
  1. Orangutan – Juvenile literature
  I. Title II. Barnham, Kay
  599.8'83

ISBN: 0 7502 4231 0

Printed and bound in Hong Kong

Hodder Children's Books
A division of Hodder Headline Limited
338 Euston Road, London NW1 3BH

Produced in association with WWF-UK.
WWF-UK registered charity number 1081247.
A company limited by guarantee number 4016725.
Panda device © 1986 WWF ® WWF registered trademark owner.

The website addresses (URLs) included in this book were valid at
the time of going to press. However, because of the nature of the
Internet, it is possible that some addresses may have changed, or
sites may have changed or closed down since publication. While
the author, packager and Publisher regret any inconvenience this
may cause readers, no responsibility for any such changes can be
accepted by either the author, packager or the publisher.

Contents

Where orangutans live

Orangutans live on the islands of Borneo and Sumatra in Asia.

They are the only members of the **great ape** family
that spend most of their time in the trees of the
rainforest. Orangutan means 'person of the forest'.

Baby orangutans

When an orangutan is born, it is small and helpless like a human baby.

The baby orangutan will drink milk from
its mother until it is about three and a half
years old. Then it starts to eat other food.

Looking after the baby

A baby orangutan stays close to
its mother, often riding on her back.

Orangutan mothers are very caring.
They protect their babies from danger and
groom them to make sure they are clean.

Family life

Mothers and babies stay together in small, friendly groups until the babies are big enough to live on their own.

Male orangutans live alone. They will fight with other males to keep control of their **territory** and the females who live there.

Learning and playing

The young orangutans learn from their
mothers how to behave and what to eat.

They play games with one another. This helps
them to grow strong. They get to know the
forest and learn how to survive there.

Getting around

Orangutans can swing through the trees by hooking their long, thin hands and feet over the branches.

When they are on the ground, orangutans walk using their hands and feet.

Eating...

Orangutans eat mainly plant food, such as fruit, leaves, bark and flowers. They pick the food as they swing through the trees.

Orangutans are very fond of fruit. They use their
fingers and thumbs to peel and eat it like we do.

...and drinking

Orangutans get most of their water by eating plants, or by licking rainwater from leaves or from their wet fur.

They also collect water from tree hollows
and rivers, by scooping up the water and
licking their wet, hairy wrists.

Resting

Searching for food, and eating it,
takes up most of the orangutan's day.

Each night, an orangutan makes
a leafy nest high up in a tree,
ready for a well-earned sleep.

The clever orangutan

Like all the great apes, orangutans are very intelligent. They can make tools from sticks to get food out of narrow spaces, or to scratch their backs.

Some orangutans have also been taught to communicate with people using **sign language**.

Threats...

Much of the orangutan's forest home is being destroyed. People cut down the trees and sell them, and then they plant new crops in their place.

In some places oil palm trees are planted.
The oil from them can be sold to make
money. Farmers often shoot orangutans when
they catch them eating the young trees.

...and dangers

Some baby orangutans are sold **illegally** as pets. Unfortunately, people cannot cope with them when they grow up.

These orangutans are being helped by people
to learn how to live in the forest again. It is
difficult for the orangutans because they have
not learned how to find food for themselves.

Helping orangutans to survive

Encouraging tourists to come to see wildlife is
a better way for local people to earn money
than by selling baby orangutans for pets.

Orangutans can live more safely in these
protected areas of forest. Here they have
enough space to find the food they need.

Further information

Find out more about how we can help orangutans in the future.

ORGANIZATIONS TO CONTACT

WWF-UK
Panda House, Weyside Park,
Godalming, Surrey GU7 1XR
Tel: 01483 426444
Website: http://www.wwf.org.uk

Orangutan Foundation International
822 S.Wellesley Avenue
Los Angeles
CA 90049
USA
Tel: 001 310 207 1655
http://www.orangutan.org

Orangutan Foundation UK
7 Kent Terrace
London NW1 4RP
Tel: 020 7724 2912
http://www.orangutan.org.uk

BOOKS

The Orangutan – Forest Acrobat
(Animal Close-ups): Christine Sourd,
Charlesbridge Publishing 2001.

Little Sibu – An Orangutan Tale
(story book): Sally Grindley,
Peachtree Publishing 1999.

Orangutans: Mae Woods, Abdo Publishing
Company 1998.

Monkeys and Apes (Animal Close-ups):
Barbara Taylor, McGraw-Hill Children's
Publishing 2002.

Glossary

WEBSITES

Most young children will need adult help when visiting websites. Those listed have child-friendly pages to bookmark.

http://www.rainforestlive.org.uk
Go to Kidz to find out about rainforests and why they should be saved.

http://www.geoimagery.com/publishers/King.html
The story, in pictures, of the rehabilitation of an orangutan called King.

great ape – the animal family that includes chimpanzees, gorillas, bonobos and orangutans.

groom – to clean fur by picking out dirt and insects.

illegally – against the law.

protected areas – safe places where wild animals can live freely.

rainforest – forests in hot, moist places.

sign language – using hands and gestures instead of talking.

territory – the home area of an animal.

31

Index